Will you 52?

Will you 52?

Living a Life of
Praise, Prayer, and Thanks

Cynthia A. Gipson Lee

DEDICATION

For my FamiLee

ACKNOWLEDGMENTS

My church family of First Baptist Church of Lincoln Gardens, Pastor and First Lady Soaries – thanks for your guidance and tutelage over the years; I've grown tremendously

Ministry Incubators & PTSEM Hatch-a-thon – thanks for providing direction on how to grow 52TY beyond the idea stage

Girlfriends Pray Life Camp/Abundant Life Camp – thanks for the content and community which helps me live BOLDLY in God's promises

My 52TY Team – thanks for helping to shape this project; let's gear up for what God is bringing next

My trianGLR & DigitaLee families – thanks for your support; no matter the idea, you've always been there to say "You can do it!"

My FamiLee – thanks for giving so freely of yourselves to assist me in completing these goals

My sister, Sonia – thanks for being by my side for it all

My parents – thanks for laying a solid foundation of faith in my life and continuously nurturing my creativity

My kids: Aja, Chinor II, and Zacharias – thanks for your encouragement which helps me to push forward and try new things

My husband, Chinor – thanks for providing the "Yes, And" for my many BIG ideas; I couldn't have done any of this without your support throughout all aspects of my life

My list of 52 (and counting) – thanks for pouring into me

Everyone who has ever prayed for me – I thank you

intro

QUESTION

Over the hill. That was the saying we used when I was growing up for anyone turning 40. As a kid, 40 seemed so old. No longer could you watch Saturday morning cartoons or be excited about back-to-back episodes of Batman and Superman. You. Were. 40! What lay ahead was a life of coffee, Cream of Wheat and reading the "funny pages" for a laugh. Oh, and don't forget a big birthday party where your closest friends and family celebrate you getting old by adorning a room with black streamers, "Over the Hill" paraphernalia, and a fake cane for good measure.

As life continued and the years started to add on, 30 didn't seem quite that old, and 40, nah, that didn't look the same. Through the eyes of a kid to that of a 38-year-old, the closer I got to that "magic number," my view changed from an "Over the Hill" mantra to that of "Forty and Fabulous" touted across the Party City aisles.

Approaching my 40th birthday, I wanted to celebrate in some significant way. My husband, Chinor, turned 40 a year ahead of me, and we had an incredible celebration for him full of fun and food, and to top it off, we had a caricature artist come over and do sketches of everyone at the party. We all loved it! As my 39th birthday drew near, I was asked: "Next year is the big one...what do you want to do?" While on its surface this question was asking how I wanted to celebrate, I took it as what is something special that I want to do to mark my 40th year and make it different from each year leading up to it.

Chinor had a theme of 4 for 40 and set out to complete four obstacle course races through the year. He crushed that goal and was finishing up his 7th event! What an inspiration! So, what does this mean to me? I had two choices.

1. Congratulate him and move on or
2. Use it as motivation

LISTEN

I couldn't get these questions out of my head. Not long after, I was out walking one morning in my neighborhood; I often take this time to get away from all the digital noise I consume and talk to God. The original music from the birds along my path helps me to center in on God's majesty. After thanking God for the day and praying for my health, our conversation started to focus on that looming question. What birthday goal do I have for myself?

My mind went back to my 30th birthday. I set out to give my family handwritten thank-you cards at my party as appreciation for all they did for me over the years. I went to the store, bought the cards...but never wrote them. This was almost ten years ago!

Me: *Alright, God, so am I dusting that idea off? Maybe I can attempt the thank-you notes (again). There would be just a few people in the family coming over for my 40th birthday party next year. I could handle those thank you cards.*

God: *52.*

Me: *Huh? What'd you say, God? Right, so I'll write probably like 12 cards to cover everyone. Chinor, Mom & Pop, the kids, Ma, Rankins, Hayes, Joshuas, Clarkes, Gipsons, Underwoods, Uncle Bill…man, this is adding UP!*

God: 52.

Me: *Ok, how about, I do 20? 30? Alright, fine. 40 for 40. That's catchy. Forty people will be REALLY hard to pull off, but hey, I'll give it a try.*

God: 52.

Me: *C'mon! Isn't 40 close enough? I won't even have that many people coming to my party!*

God: 52.

Me: *Maaaybe you forgot this was Cynthia, God. Your daughter who has "good intentions" but doesn't have the best track record in following through. You DO remember me buying the cards ten years ago and never doing anything with them. Right? How am I supposed to do 52?*

Then, God laid it on me to do one per week for the whole year. Take it in steps. *I'll be with you.* The more I walked and talked with God, my skepticism turned to delight as we brainstormed and came up with not just giving a note, but praying for the person as I wrote it. Praise, prayer, and thanks are how I would do my thank yous. That's how 52 Thank Yous was born.

BEGIN

Excitement rushed through me as I went into planning mode; which I LOVE to do. I worked out the mechanics behind the idea and how I would approach each week. I designed a logo, created the thank you cards, made a list of 52 people and randomized it. Then, I got ready for the kick-off day of my 39th birthday. This project was top secret. I didn't tell anyone what God and I had cooked up. I wanted it to be a surprise for each person as they received their card in the mail.

I started the work of the first person, then the next, and the next. Each week was a blessing for me as I was praying and connecting with these people who have poured so much into my life. Things were going quite well. I progressed from October through December smoothly. Before crossing over into the New Year, I took some time to review my previous goals/activities for that year and was reminded of a conference I wanted to attend.

< DREAMY MUSIC + FLASHBACK >

I saw a program at Princeton Theological Seminary called the Hatch-a-thon. I have a software background and have participated in Hackathons before where you spend all night writing code and have a novel product (hopefully!) to show at the end of it. This conference from the Ministry Incubators was like a Hackathon except for ministerial ideas. If you had a dream for some new social or missional innovation, that 3-day conference was the place to dive in and spend dedicated time to write the vision and make it plain. I was enamored by the concept and wanted to be there. However, I didn't have any burning ideas of what I would present. After a while, my window of opportunity began to close, and I started to divert the money elsewhere. No Hatch-a-thon for me. :-(

As I worked my 52 (translation: completed my list one week at a time) and got feedback from people who received the thank you cards, I saw it as something that was blessing them as well as growing me. Here I was about 12 months after first seeing the Hatch-a-thon, and God spoke it again. This idea! It had already been crossing my mind that 52 Thank Yous (52TY) is something that others would benefit from doing for themselves. God opened a door for me to be at the Hatch-a-thon, and I ran through it. AMAZING!!!

LEAN IN

Over the next few months, I continued moving through my 52 and began to prepare for the upcoming Hatch-a-thon with my dad (I call him Pop). Though he had a phenomenal ministry product that he designed, developed and had been selling, he decided to come in as a partner with me. We've done a few of these start-up programs together, and I was doubly excited about this one. Now I got to combine my love for innovation with my desire to be of service in God's Kingdom.

Initially, writing a book wasn't even on our radar. Pop and I went in with some goals of sharing the idea, helping it become a ministry so others can use it themselves, and create support products like notecards and guides to help people along their journey. Since we both had technical backgrounds, we were also looking to develop an app so people could monitor their 52TY "on-the-go." As we got deeper into our planning and received feedback from other participants, our immediate goals shifted, and just as God continued to speak, we saw how this idea fit so well with a book. Not necessarily a book where it would describe my own 52 Thank Yous journey, but rather something that would help teach others.

WIN - WIN

For the past few years, I've had an urge to write. I knew this urge is something from God because it is so far from my personality. I started the year writing about an entirely different topic. However, that got put on hold as 52 Thank Yous began to grow. My gift to others turned out to be a gift for me as well.

It was clear that the 52-week journey was not something that I could do on my own. I was a chronic procrastinator, my schedule was often fully loaded, and I had a hard time being disciplined in MANY areas of my life. It was only through God's power working in me that I was able to achieve this goal. That's not to say that I didn't have any hiccups, where I *may* have written a stack of cards all at once, or I prayed for my "last week" person the same time I was praying for my "this week" person. The point was, in the past, I'd run into a bad week and after beating myself up would completely stop my plan. However, this time was much different. God assigned me a person of the week. I now had a name and a face of someone I love and appreciate that I needed to pray for. That helped me to push past where the "old Cynthia" would've gotten off, so that I could keep going to the next stop and the next stop, with God by my side. Thank you, God!

There was a devotion I read in Our Daily Bread many years ago titled "Surprise Me!" The message that stood out to me was asking if I trusted God enough with the life that I was given to ask God to surprise me. Initially, we may quickly say, "Of Course!" because who doesn't like surprises. But, after taking a beat to reflect a little longer, I realized that for God to bring me somewhere new, I had to leave a lot of this old stuff behind. God's not going to give me time to go home and pack a bag. No. When God says "Move", I need to be ready to move. *Whatever You give me, wherever you lead me, is beyond all that I could think or even imagine for myself.* I've prayed that "Surprise Me" prayer many times before, and have been blown away by what God did in me, for me, and through me. When I lean into God, when YOU lean into God and see where it is that God will bring you, it's just a marvelous journey.

In a style similar to that of Paul and his epistles to churches such as Ephesus and Philippi, 52 Thank Yous strives to strengthen relationships through weekly praise, prayer, and thanks for those whom God has blessed us with. As a 52er I spend my week praising God for a specific person, praying for them in targeted areas and then sending a note to thank them for blessing me. 52...to live thoughtfully and purposefully every week, every day, and every moment. Will you 52?

GETTING STARTED

I am the
Lord your
God WHO
TEACHES
YOU what
is good for

you

Isaiah 48:17 NLT

HOW TO USE THE BOOK

This study guide is divided into five main lessons – Praise, Prayer, Intercessory Prayer, Thanks and 52 Thank Yous. While I encourage its use as part of a small group/Bible Study class, it can be used as an individual study, as well. If it is done as a group, I would suggest studying one lesson per week and then gathering once again after completing the book to discuss your first week of 52 Thank Yous.

Each lesson starts with a memory verse. Here's a bonus one: Psalm 119:11. This is followed by a personal story from my life that serves to highlight the objective of the lesson. I encourage you to look at your own life and reflect on experiences that God reveals to you.

The sessions include discussion/reflective questions and readings from the Word which focus on the topic. There are group activities as well as individual work that seeks to enhance your spiritual and mental critical thinking skills. Lessons close with a short activity for later and introspective questions on how you will respond to the message by actions you want to stop, start or continue.

Incorporated into this study are bonus sections on the topics of praise, prayer, and thanks. These include work that can be done over the course of the week focusing on a Bible story, song, and scripture.

I've also included additional resources at the back of the book, once your 52 Thank Yous journey begins. Some being tools on How to 52 and journal pages as you step through your full list of people. Thanks for joining me on this journey through praise, prayer, and thanks.

LESSON 1
PRAISE

There is no **one**
like You & there
is no **God**
but You.

2 Samuel 7:22

Highlights

- Learn from David
- See the purpose in praising God
- Reflect on how you praise

praise is what I do

LIFE LESSON ON PRAISE

There was a time when my work life was incredibly stressful. When I was 10 years old, I wanted to be a software engineer/programmer, and I nurtured that love through high school, postgraduate studies and then into the workforce. I enjoyed the team of people that I worked with, my commute was under 15 minutes, and the work that I did came naturally. All was good.

Then, it happened...

We received new management that in a nutshell, did not manage people well. They opted for fear, intimidation, and belittlement instead of the spirit of teamwork that had previously existed. The office became a point of misery for most, and about 90% of the people in my group talked about retiring or just quitting. This was not a productive atmosphere for me. The joy that I used to get from being a part of this close-knit team began to unravel faster than a spool of thread falling off of the counter.

Initially, my prayers were for God to help ME out of the situation. *Get me out of this office!* Then I realized that those prayers would bless me but my peers and the success of our work wouldn't be made better. Being God's child, I felt compelled to look at the bigger picture and grow from "me" to "we." So, my mindset and my prayers changed to ask God to improve the situation for everyone. I began to pray for my manager and their manager, that God would bless their lives. I'd speak joy and peace not only for me but each person in my group. Though work was stressful and tempers were high, I would smile inside knowing the worse off this situation was looking, the messier it got...God would show out even more. My mind didn't know how things could get better, but my faith assured me it would.

My manager and their manager both ended up retiring within a month of each other and seemed genuinely happy with the direction of their new journey. The new manager brought to work directly with our group was a previous member of the team who had a fantastic rapport with us and extensive knowledge of our products. I knew that this major shift which completely altered the dynamics of our work environment was nothing but God.

Praising God despite the struggle was my priority. I praised God in the mess, and God made it better than alright.

Discussion Questions

What is praise?

_____

_____

_____

_____

Reflect on a time when you were praised. What was the situation? Who did it come from? How did you feel?

_____

_____

_____

_____

Let's think about the praise we give to a co-worker or children vs. that which we give to God. When we *praise* people, we often praise them for what they've done.
- *Great job on that customer meeting.*
- *Wow, look how clean your room is. Awesome!*

We frequently correlate this praise with congratulations. Often when I think of God, my mind goes to things that God has done - woke me up, blessed my family, and gave me resources. But, God doesn't have to do one more thing, to deserve my praise – our praise. Let's praise God for who God is!

GOD IS...

When you think of God, what adjectives come to mind?

_____

_____

_____

_____

The book of Psalms has many praises to God. Dig into the Word and list some reasons in these passages where David stated why we should praise God.

Psalm 23   _____

Psalm 100   _____

Psalm 121   _____

Now, find some of your own in a different chapter.

_____   _____

_____   _____

60-second challenge

 In a group or solo, complete the sentence aloud "God is ___." Go round-robin style with everyone sharing an answer. Speed it up! Now do a 30 second round, then a 10 second round.

PURPOSE IN PRAISE

Posture
God is sovereign. When we humble ourselves before God, giving God all of the glory, it allows for us to adjust our posture. Come to God correctly.
PSALM 149:4-5; 1 PETER 5:6; JAMES 4:10

Presence
God is everywhere. Praise helps us acknowledge God's presence in this place.
PSALM 140:13; JAMES 4:8A

Priorities
God is #1. Praise helps align our priorities and put God first.
MATTHEW 6:33

How do you praise?

_____

_____

_____

ACTION

When I was in elementary school, I remember getting an assignment where students needed to create an acrostic for their name – listing a characteristic for each letter. I often did this:

CYNTHIA
Creative, **Y**oung, **N**ice, **T**all*, **H**appy, **I**ntelligent, **A**rtistic

*Back in the 2nd grade, I felt like a tall kid. Who would've known years later that I'd only grow to be 4' 11"? Ha!

Let's create an acrostic for God. Think of characteristics of God going by your name. Think about this in relation to you. God created you. God made you who you are. God knows all about you. So, when you look at yourself and look at your name, spell this out and think about characteristics of God that start with those letters.

Sometime during this next week, search the Word and find evidence as to that trait of God.

Letter	Characteristic	Evidence
_____	_____	_____
_____	_____	_____
_____	_____	_____
_____	_____	_____
_____	_____	_____
_____	_____	_____
_____	_____	_____
_____	_____	_____
_____	_____	_____

DEEPER DIVE

Looking at the morning sky and the evening sky. What are some things that come to mind as you think of God? God's majesty; God's creativity. Try to distinguish between praising God for these things as opposed to thanking God for something.

Stop | Start | Continue

As a takeaway from today's lesson on praise, what is something that you will commit to do this week? Based on today's lesson, I want to:

Stop _____

Start _____

Continue _____

PRAYER

There is no one like You, God. Thank you for loving me through the times where I lose sight of You. Please help me keep my focus on You and gain a richer praise experience.

Write your own prayer:

_____

_____

_____

_____

_____

NOTES

PRAISE BONUS

I will *praise* you with an upright heart

Psalm 119:7

STORY

People often say that prayer changes things. I'll contend praise also has that effect. 2 Chronicles depicts a battle which was won through praise. Read 2 Chronicles 13:1- 23 to learn more about the battle.

How did Jehoshaphat show through his prayers he was really talking to the Lord?

_____

_____

_____

_____

In verse 21, why is praise and declaration of God's greatness so important during times of crisis?

_____

_____

_____

_____

Have you ever encountered a situation that overwhelmed your resources? How did you respond?

_____

_____

_____

_____

SONG

List some songs that speak to you on **praise**:

- _____
- _____
- _____
- _____

Choose one of these songs, and jot down some lyrics that stand out to you.

_____
_____
_____
_____
_____

Is this song based on any scripture? If so, list below:

- _____
- _____
- _____

How do you feel when you hear/sing/play this song?

_____
_____
_____
_____

SCRIPTURE

Stand on the Word. Look up **Hebrews 13:15** in different
translations. Highlight the common words or themes.

Translation 1 _____

_____

_____

_____

_____

Translation 2 _____

_____

_____

_____

_____

Translation 3 _____

_____

_____

_____

_____

Rewrite this scripture in your own words.

_____

_____

_____

_____

LESSON 2
PRAYER

Whatever you ask in prayer,
believe that you have received
it, and it will be yours.

Mark 11:24

Highlights

- Learn from Jesus
- See the power in prayer to God
- Reflect on how you pray

prayer made the difference

LIFE LESSON ON PRAYER

I loved hearing the gospel songs my parents would play when I was growing up and would loudly sing along with my sister, Sonia – in the car, around the house, anywhere and everywhere! The song "I Found Out" by Danniebelle Hall was one that I particularly liked. However, when I pushed past the catchy beat and listened more attentively as an adult, I got checked by my Spirit. She talked about changing her ways from consistently begging God for a laundry list of requests, to instead give God praise. She found that by making praise a priority, other things in life began to get better. Wow. Here I was, day after day, often spending time in prayer to ASK God for stuff, but not focusing on the relationship building portion of prayer.

I likened this to a scene that often happens between kids and their parents. Let's say a teenager wants to go to the movies after school and stay out a little past curfew. Oh, and to do this, they'd need a ride to the theater. Aaaand their friend needs a ride too. "Can I also have money for popcorn because I only have enough for the ticket?"

As a parent, if you start to hear a list like this, the answer could quickly be a NO after the second "Can I..." However, it may be a different story if the child said:

Hi, Mom and Dad. How are you? You know, you two are the best. So loving, caring, nurturing. I know I don't make it easy for you sometimes in raising me with the moods I get into, or times I walk into the house and ignore you, but you love me anyway. Thanks for that, and all of the advice you give me. Especially on making good choices in life and surrounding myself with positive people. I was wondering, in the spirit of friendship, can I ...?

Doesn't that sound different? Of course, we'd probably give or get a side-eye when all of the flattery was being laid out, knowing an ask was around the corner. But, isn't it a blessing that God isn't like us? ☺ God LOVES our praise; LOVES our attention. LOVES when we don't just walk around the world acting like God didn't create it for us...or isn't here...or didn't breathe life into us. When we come to God, our Creator, our Sustainer, our EVERYTHING, we need to come correctly.

DISCUSSION QUESTIONS

What is prayer?

_____

_____

_____

How does prayer make you feel? After you've prayed? After someone prayed for you?

_____

_____

_____

_____

Prayer is a doorway for us to talk to God. These dedicated conversations with God, our Creator, allows us to build a substantial relationship by spending time with one another. Prayer is that personalized time with God and me.

JESUS' LESSON

Jesus was often found praying in the Bible. Read Matthew 6:7 – 14 aloud to see the lesson Jesus gave on how we should pray.

A simple way to look at prayer is to divide it into four parts – ACTS.

Adoration	I love you
Confession	I'm sorry
Thanks	I thank you
Supplication	Help me/others

Read the Lord's Prayer again with these in mind, and identify portions for each category:

A _____

C _____

T _____

S _____

Similar to the life lesson above, many times when we pray, we immediately go to the "S" in ACTS and start listing off things we'd like God to do for us. Sure, there are times when all we can do is call out to God for help at that moment. However, let's not make that our only kind of prayer. Don't miss out on the blessings that come from the full model Jesus gave.

60-second challenge

In a group, go around and share an example for each letter of ACTS. Each person will first share something they love about God. Then, go around the circle and share something you are sorry for (doesn't have to be personal), an example may be wasting time. The next rotation would be something you thank God for, and then finish up with something you are asking God for.

POWER IN PRAYER

Perspective
Prayer gives us perspective by helping us take the focus off us (our problems/issues) and put it on God. Prayer allows us one-on-one time with God.
MATTHEW 6:6

Primary
Prayer is never secondary; it's always primary. It's not the last recourse when options run out; it's our first and best resource.
EPHESIANS 6:13, 17-20

Peace
Prayer grants us hope and peace in times of trouble. While focusing on God and all God can do, we get an assurance that God will give us calm hearts and minds.
PHILIPPIANS 4:6-7

Are there some things you don't take to God in prayer? Why?

_____

_____

_____

_____

ACTION

As Matthew walked along with Jesus, he noted a few lessons on prayer. Read the scriptures and see what Jesus said. Summarize in your own words.

Matthew 5:44

_____

_____

_____

Matthew 21:22

_____

_____

_____

Matthew 26:41

_____

_____

_____

In Matthew 6:5-6, Jesus gave a preamble to the Lord's Prayer. Note some tips from the scripture.

_____

_____

_____

DEEPER DIVE

This week, choose one of those things you've been holding back from God and pray about it.

Stop | Start | Continue

As a takeaway from today's lesson on prayer, what is something you will commit to do this week? Based on today's lesson, I want to:

Stop _____

Start _____

Continue _____

PRAYER

God, You are the Source of my strength. I often try and do things my way and make a mess, but you lovingly guide me back onto Your Path. Thanks for giving me a lamp for my feet and a light for my pathway. Please help me stay in communion and conversation with You so I can build a more vibrant prayer life.

Write your own prayer:

_____

_____

_____

_____

_____

NOTES

LESSON 3
INTERCESSORY PRAYER

And the Holy Spirit *helps us in our weakness. We don't know what God wants us to pray for. But the Holy Spirit* prays *for us with groanings that* **cannot be expressed in words.**

Romans 8:26 NLT

Highlights

- Learn from the Holy Spirit

- Practice praying for others

- Reflect on how you can intercede for others

somebody prayed for me

LIFE LESSON ON INTERCESSORY PRAYER

Our family was going through some significant life
changes. My husband felt God's nudge and
began attending seminary full-time after a
whirlwind year of finding his dream career and gaining a
wealth of rewarding work experiences. Trying our best to
be obedient, we bravely marched forward and made it
through the first year. Phew! There were only two years left
to go however we had immediately felt the pressure of
being down to one income. We couldn't keep this up
without a monumental change.

The seminary was building new campus housing which
would be open for applications the following fall. We
already had a house 4-towns over and wondered do we
sell or stay. It was becoming hard to keep up the payments
on the house and all that comes along with home
ownership. However, making our home market-ready
would require a significant investment in updates and
repairs. Do we invest the money for those? Is there even a
vacancy in the new apartments? What if we put the house
on the market, and it sells, but we don't get the campus
housing? What if the house doesn't sell but we already
"sunk" all of this money into the updates...can we keep up
with other bills? How would the kids adjust to a move? With
each question that raced through my mind, I felt like I was

losing control of this steady ship we'd been steering for the past few years. I tried not to dump all of my worries at Chinor's feet because I wanted him to be able to focus on school. And, how could I bring family and friends into this and have them know that we were short on money? I began to be consumed by this avalanche of "what ifs" which threatened my family.

At that time, the song I was playing in heavy rotation in my car was "In the Midst of it All" by Yolanda Adams. That song reminded me of God's provision, Jesus' love, and the Holy Spirit's peace. We looked back at all that God brought us through and knew that God would continue to carry us forward. So, we decided to put the house on the market.

To me, this was one of those bold "God's Got It" type of decisions, so one day, I started it by fasting and asked family from all over to join a call for a quick lunchtime prayer. Whereas I initially wanted to hide our private struggles, we instead embraced God's resources of family, community, and prayer to bring about a change.

Over the next 30 minutes, we prayed for not just our situation, but anything else that folks on the line needed. About a week later, we were talking through email about how impactful our prayer time was and how we wanted to do it more. Out of that "Our Praying Family" was born. We came together roughly once a month for family prayer on themes and specific requests. People on both sides of mine and my husband's family have joined over the years. It's amazing how God brings to life new things even in the midst of our struggle.

Discussion Questions

Have you ever gotten to the point where you have a hard time praying for something? How did this make you feel?

_____

_____

_____

_____

When we can't utter the words; when we can't even settle our minds on what to pray for, the Holy Spirit is interceding for us - just as Jesus does. Read Romans 8:26-27.

How do you feel after reading this?

_____

_____

_____

_____

In the same way that the Holy Spirit intercedes for us daily, we are urged to pray and intercede for others in 1 Timothy 2:1.

Has anyone ever interceded on your behalf? (Not only by prayer, but other means as well.) How did it make you feel?

_____

_____

_____

_____

Have you been asked to pray for someone? Describe the experience (details aren't necessary).

_____

_____

_____

_____

2-minute challenge

Pair off and pray. Spend 30 seconds telling your partner about yourself. Your partner will then pray for 30 seconds for you. Switch.
If you are doing this study alone, phone a friend and do this quick exercise with them.

Reflect on both sides of this workout experience.

Giving a prayer

_____

_____

_____

_____

Receiving a prayer

_____

_____

_____

_____

ACTION

Read James 5:13 – 16.   Share your thoughts below on the passage regarding intercessory prayer.

_____

_____

_____

Find your own example from the Bible where someone interceded on behalf of another. Describe the situation.
Examples: Genesis 24:1-26; Nehemiah 1: 3-11

Scripture Reference   _____

Who Interceded?   _____

For Whom?   _____

_____

_____

_____

_____

_____

_____

DEEPER DIVE

Pray for your partner in the class sometime later this week.

Stop | Start | Continue

As a takeaway from today's lesson on intercessory prayer, what is something you will commit to do this week? Based on today's lesson, I want to:

Stop _____

Start _____

Continue _____

PRAYER

God, You are Love. Thanks for sharing your love with me, and blessing me with others in my life I can love as well. Please help me to love as Jesus did so I can pray for others. Bring people to my Spirit that need an extra smile and always keep me ready to serve.

Write your own prayer:

_____

_____

_____

_____

_____

NOTES

PRAYER BONUS

If you **REMAIN IN ME** *and my words remain in you, ask whatever you wish, and it will be done for you.*

John 15:7

STORY

These are accounts of some prayers in the Bible.

Hezekiah's Prayer   2 Kings 19:14 - 19
Hannah's Prayer   1 Samuel 2:1-10
David's Prayer   1 Chronicles 17:15 - 27

What do you think of when you read Hezekiah's Prayer?

_____

_____

_____

Hannah's Prayer?

_____

_____

_____

David's Prayer?

_____

_____

_____

What can you learn from their situations?

_____

_____

_____

SONG

List some songs that speak to you on **prayer**:

- _____
- _____
- _____
- _____

Choose one of these songs, and jot down some lyrics that stand out to you.

_____
_____
_____
_____
_____

Is this song based on any scripture? If so, list below:

- _____
- _____
- _____

How do you feel when you hear/sing/play this song?

_____
_____
_____
_____

SCRIPTURE

Stand on the Word.   Look up **Philippians 4:6** in different translations. Highlight the common words or themes.

Translation 1 _____

_____

_____

_____

_____

Translation 2 _____

_____

_____

_____

_____

Translation 3 _____

_____

_____

_____

_____

Rewrite this scripture in your own words.

_____

_____

_____

_____

LESSON 4
THANKS

I will give thanks
to You, Lord, with
all my heart.

Psalm 9:1

Highlights

- Learn from the choir

- See how we can find triumph in giving thanks
  to God

- Reflect on how you give thanks

I really am grateful

MEMORY VERSE

Remember what Christ taught, and let his words enrich your lives and make you wise; teach them to each other and sing them out in psalms and hymns and spiritual songs, singing to the Lord with thankful hearts.

COLOSSIANS 3:16 TLB

LIFE LESSON ON THANKS

As a kid, I used to complain...a LOT! Unfortunately, that practice carried on into my early adulthood. At the office, when I would be around co-workers, I'd join in (or often start) the complaining about busyness, pay, vacation days, etc. At times, I'd catch myself, not wanting to be the one always saying, "Oh, I never have any money," or I don't like this or that. But, that self-check didn't always stick.

This changed at my grandmother's funeral. I remember hearing my dad give the eulogy where he shared that one of my Grandma's favorite songs was "I Won't Complain." That was like a gut punch from my Spirit. My God. Here I was going through life nit-picking on all of the "bad." It's not that I didn't appreciate the good, but if someone from the outside only caught one sound-bite from me, would they know how God's blessed me? From that moment, the spirit of complaining was gone. The way I combatted it was by being thankful. God's done WAY too much for me, for anything other than praise and thanksgiving to come from my lips.

DISCUSSION QUESTIONS

How did you show thanks to God today?

_____

_____

_____

_____

GRATITUDE FOR GOD

Read Psalm 136:1-9. As many of the psalms are songs, I imagined a choir performing this passage during a morning service. The lead singer belting out the first portion, and the choir adding in "His love endures forever."

How do you feel after reading this?

_____

_____

_____

_____

When you think of being grateful and thankful, do you see those as the same? What are some similarities? Differences?

_____

_____

_____

_____

Initially, I didn't put much thought into if they were the same or not. Then, one Sunday, our choir was singing "Grateful" by Hezekiah Walker. With each utterance of the word "grateful" that we sung, I began to see these words differently. I started looking at the word "thankful" as something that I could do, but someone did for me instead. However, being grateful was much more profound. Gratefulness is being thankful for something only God can do.

60-second challenge

 Think about a pen or pencil that you may have in front of you. List as many reasons as you can to be thankful to God for it. After the time is up, do a group share.

List reasons below

_____

_____

_____

_____

What was it like to thank God for a pen/pencil?

_____

_____

_____

_____

TRIUMPH IN THANKS

Think
Giving thanks allows us to take thought for the comfort and the good of others.
EPHESIANS 1:16

Transform

No matter what is going on or how challenging the circumstances of our lives, we can always find something to give thanks for. In so doing, we can take the focus off what is "not working."
1 THESSALONIANS 5:18

Testify

Proclaim God's goodness. Give thanks for what God is doing, has done, and will do.
1 CHRONICLES 16:8-9

How do you *show* God that you are thankful?

_____

_____

_____

_____

ACTION

I remember learning that the way that I'm blessed is through other people operating in their gifts. God increases me, strengthens me, and blesses me through other people. That's the same way I should look to serve, give and be gracious to people; by using my gifts. My gifts and skills are given to me to bless others. I am grateful for God putting them in my life.

Reflecting on gratitude/thankfulness helps to put life in perspective so that we don't hold ourselves higher than we ought. We don't do/accomplish anything on our own. Thankfulness helps us to reflect on the importance of community, family, friendships and being amongst people.

Read Philippians 4:10 – 20.

Reflect on a time where someone has blessed you in the way Paul was blessed.

_____

_____

_____

_____

Deeper Dive

Read the rest of Psalm 136 and summarize what the song is thanking God for.

Psalm 136:10 – 15

_____

_____

_____

Psalm 136:16 – 22

_____

_____

_____

Psalm 136:23 – 26

_____

_____

_____

Stop | Start | Continue

As a takeaway from today's lesson on thanks, what is something you will commit to do this week? Based on today's lesson, I want to:

Stop _____

Start _____

Continue _____

PRAYER

> If I had a thousand tongues, I couldn't thank You enough! You supply me with all my needs and even bless me with many of my "wants." I know that I often take your blessings for granted. Please help me to slow down and make the time to delight in You. You are a marvelous God!

Write your own prayer:

_____

_____

_____

_____

_____

NOTES

THANKS BONUS

But thanks be to God! He gives us the victory through our Lord Jesus Christ.

I Corinthians 15:57

Story

Read Luke 17:11 – 19 about Jesus healing the ten lepers.

What does the action of the foreigner (and Jesus' response) teach us?

_____

_____

_____

_____

Why is it important to give thanks to God?

_____

_____

_____

_____

Why do you think the foreigner was so much more thankful than the other lepers?

_____

_____

_____

What is something you haven't thanked God for? Why?

_____

_____

_____

_____

SONG

List some songs that speak to you on **thanks**:

- _____
- _____
- _____
- _____

Choose one of these songs, and jot down some lyrics that stand out to you.

_____
_____
_____
_____
_____

Is this song based on any scripture? If so, list below:

- _____
- _____
- _____

How do you feel when you hear/sing/play this song?

_____
_____
_____
_____

SCRIPTURE

Stand on the Word. Look up **Hebrews 12:28** in different translations. Highlight the common words or themes.

Translation 1 _____

_____

_____

_____

_____

Translation 2 _____

_____

_____

_____

_____

Translation 3 _____

_____

_____

_____

_____

Rewrite this scripture in your own words.

_____

_____

_____

_____

LESSON 5
52 THANK YOUS

I always thank my God
for you and for the gracious
gifts He has given you.

I Corinthians 1:4 NLT

Highlights

- Learn from Paul

- Practice the components of 52TY

- Prepare for the journey

how do I say thank you

Pray in the Spirit at all times and on every occasion. Stay alert and be persistent in your prayers for all believers everywhere.

EPHESIANS 6:18 NLT

LIFE LESSON ON 52 THANK YOUS

I was preparing a lesson for this book and was searching in the Bible for verses on various topics. While navigating here and there through the scripture, I found something that just floored me.

1 Thessalonians 5:17 is a verse that I know well -- "Pray without ceasing." We use this in Bible Study to answer the question "When do we pray?". Answer: Always! Since I had been studying these epistles from Paul, I backed up a little and read from verse 12, when Paul was giving some final instructions. Coming to verse 16, I saw, "Rejoice always," then "pray continually" in verse 17, and then "give thanks in all circumstances" in verse 18. Wait, what? Praise, prayer, and thanks??? My God. Here I was about 48 weeks deep into 52 Thank Yous, and now, I'm seeing in God's Word, how Paul was instructing them to give praise, prayer, and thanks for this is God's Will. This was the same message that God gave me during that early morning walk as I was working out the specifics of 52 Thank Yous.

Upon realizing this, one of my memory verses came to mind:

Do not let this Book of the Law depart from your mouth; meditate on it day and night, so that you may be careful and do everything written in it. Then you will be prosperous and successful.

Joshua 1:8

Christian meditation is a form of contemplative prayer, which usually involves focusing on and the silent repetition of scripture. Because I was in God's Word, and spending time in God's presence, I saw where my actions and plans were lining up with God's Will. Thank You, God!

DISCUSSION QUESTIONS

In Joshua 1:8, what is a necessary component for a successful life? How can you apply this to your walk?

_____

_____

_____

_____

The previous lessons have focused your study on praise, prayer, and thanks. Now, we combine these three components into 52 Thank Yous. Let's learn from Paul as he wrote many epistles/letters to churches.

Look at how Paul started his letter to the church of Ephesus, by reading Ephesians 1. Note where he gave praise, prayer, and thanks.

Praise

_____

_____

_____

Prayer

_____

_____

_____

Thanks

_____

_____

_____

2 minute (and 15 seconds) challenge

We're going to do a mini 52 Thank Yous right now.

15 seconds: Choose a person in your life

_____

30 seconds: Think about them (special memory, characteristics, etc.).

_____

_____

_____

_____

30 seconds: Praise God for creating that person and blessing you with them.

_____

_____

_____

_____

30 seconds: Pray for them.

_____

_____

_____

_____

30 seconds: Write a note to them here.

_____

_____

_____

_____

How was that? Write down some of your general thoughts.

_____

_____

_____

_____

52 Thank Yous is about committing to weekly praise, prayer and thanks for a special person to you. What are some of your strengths that can help towards a successful week?

Strengths   **How this Helps**

_____   _____

_____   _____

_____   _____

You know you. What are some potential roadblocks you may encounter which would attempt to deter your commitment for one week, four weeks, or the full 52 weeks?

Potential Hiccups   **Action Plan**

_____   _____

_____   _____

_____   _____

ACTION

What are some areas of prayer that you want to focus on for your person listed above? Find a scripture you can stand on as you pray for them.

Prayer Area   **Scripture Reference**

_____   _____

_____   _____

_____   _____

Deeper Dive

Start your 52 Thank Yous.

Stop | Start | Continue

As a takeaway from today's lesson on 52 Thanks Yous, what is something you will commit to do this week? Based on today's lesson, I want to:

Stop _____

Start _____

Continue _____

PRAYER

God, You are enough. I can rest in You, knowing that You can help me achieve goals that seem unreachable. Thanks for creating this space where I could learn more about praise, prayer, and thanks. I ask from now that You bless my journey with 52 Thank Yous. That with each person I focus on, lives will be changed –theirs and mine. I love You.

Write your own prayer:

_____

_____

_____

_____

_____

NOTES

NEXT STEPS

Whatever
you do,
work at
it with
all your
heart

Colossians 3:23

fully committed

Congratulations on completing the Will You 52? Curriculum!

You've finished Bible Study lessons on praise, prayer, thanks and how to implement these in 52 Thank Yous. From here, you start your path on 52 Thank Yous by doing your first four people. Just commit to doing one month...four weeks...one person a week. Write the names of 4 people on the list that follows. For each of them, spend your time in praise, prayer, and thanks.

Stay involved in the community of 52 Thank Yous by checking in via the website, app, email; you can even send us a real note! We just want to stay engaged with you as we encourage each other. If there are questions, wins, or lessons you've learned, we want to hear about it. Visit us online at WillYou52.com.

You can also document some of this for yourself in the journal pages we've included in the Resource Section. Here, you can expand your list of 4 people to be the full 52. It's ok to add a few at a time.

There are some journal pages as well. As you take your first person, you can write their name and some focus areas. Take notes! Journal and jot down what may be going on in your spirit as you work your 52. Then, person by person, just seek after God and notice what God will do for you. Be blessed!

expressing **gratitude** through PRAISE & prayer

HOW TO 52

Your last Bible lesson gave a quick review on how to 52. This section will supply more details. Below is a graphic used to explain 52 Thank Yous. Let's explore each section.

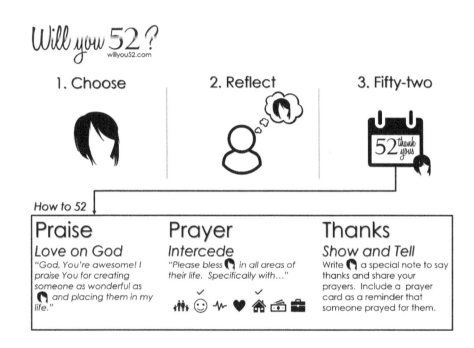

CHOOSE

There are a plethora of people you've come in contact with during your life. I started my list by thinking on those who have poured into me and helped shape me into the person God designed me to be. I also looked at others who have shown kindness to me and blessed me by doing or saying something, or just by watching how they live their lives. I put them on the list as well. I prayed God would show me the people to add. And, my list grew beyond the 52!

When it came time to take on a person for the week, I decided to choose someone randomly. This way I'm surprised at the beginning of each week, who I'll be praying for. It definitely doesn't have to be done this way. You can pick your order ahead of time, or ask God to help you choose week to week.

REFLECT

Once you pick your person of the week, spend time reflecting on their characteristics. Think about: who they are, what makes them special, and what makes them special to you. Think about how they've enriched your life and why you want to thank them. Also, choose areas in their life where you'd like to focus your prayers.

FIFTY-TWO

Planning is fantastic and helps us to organize. Now, it's time to act! With your pre-work done and your person in mind, start your 52 Thank Yous by going to God in praise, prayer, and thanks. Use what you learned in this study.

You may pray for that person on a particular day of the week. Or as you move about your days, you keep them in mind. You could incorporate it into your entire week, such that while you are at the gym, you pray for their health. And, while you commute to work, you pray for their assignment from God.

Make the time to write a special note expressing your appreciation. Yes, it could be something that fits into 280 charters or fewer. But, think of how honored someone would feel receiving a handwritten note in the mail or delivered in person.

Try multiple things and see what works. You can use some of what I listed above, come up with your own, or look to the 52TY community for ideas. The best plan is what will help you to be consistent and set you up for success.

RESOURCES

LIST

Use this to list the 52 people that you would like to pray for. Don't worry about the order. Just list the names. As you begin working, you can put which week number they are. Then, a check after you fifty-two!

		Name				**Name**
e.g. ☑	4	Chinor, 11		☑	7	Zacharias

		Name				**Name**
☐	___	_____		☐	___	_____
☐	___	_____		☐	___	_____
☐	___	_____		☐	___	_____
☐	___	_____		☐	___	_____
☐	___	_____		☐	___	_____
☐	___	_____		☐	___	_____
☐	___	_____		☐	___	_____
☐	___	_____		☐	___	_____
☐	___	_____		☐	___	_____

- [ ] ___ _____
- [ ] ___ _____
- [ ] ___ _____
- [ ] ___ _____
- [ ] ___ _____
- [ ] ___ _____
- [ ] ___ _____
- [ ] ___ _____
- [ ] ___ _____
- [ ] ___ _____
- [ ] ___ _____
- [ ] ___ _____
- [ ] ___ _____
- [ ] ___ _____
- [ ] ___ _____
- [ ] ___ _____
- [ ] ___ _____

- [ ] ___ _____
- [ ] ___ _____
- [ ] ___ _____
- [ ] ___ _____
- [ ] ___ _____
- [ ] ___ _____
- [ ] ___ _____
- [ ] ___ _____
- [ ] ___ _____
- [ ] ___ _____
- [ ] ___ _____
- [ ] ___ _____
- [ ] ___ _____
- [ ] ___ _____
- [ ] ___ _____
- [ ] ___ _____
- [ ] ___ _____

REFLECT

These pages can help organize your thoughts about your person of the week. Use the example below as a guide, but feel free to write as much or as little needed.

e.g.

Name: Aja   **Date:** 3/13

Characteristics	big heart, love for family, faithful
Special Memories	family trip to Sandy Cove; singing Dreamgirls in the car; our "failed" tubing experience along the canal ☺
Thanks	always loving me; making the most of our family time; being down to try new things
Area(s) for Prayer	education, life's path, heart's desire
Scripture Base	Jeremiah 29:11

Name: _____   **Date:** _____

Characteristics	
Special Memories	
Thanks	
Area(s) for Prayer	
Scripture Base	

Starting is often the hardest part, but you have done it! Great job. Reflect on your week below. Add one person to your 52TY list.

Worked Well	
Try This	
God showed me	

Name: **Date:**

Characteristics	
Special Memories	
Thanks	
Area(s) for Prayer	
Scripture Base	

2 Halfway to your 1-month! I knew you could do it. Add two people to your 52TY list. Share your progress with the 52TY community.

Worked Well	
Try This	
God showed me	

Name: _____   **Date:** _____

Characteristics	
Special Memories	
Thanks	
Area(s) for Prayer	
Scripture Base	

3. Three weeks and counting! You are on your way. Pray for the encouragement to go the full 52 weeks. Add three people to your 52TY list.

Worked Well	
Try This	
God showed me	

Name: **Date:**

Characteristics	
Special Memories	
Thanks	
Area(s) for Prayer	
Scripture Base	

Congrats on finishing your 4th week of 52 Thank Yous. Add four or more people to your 52TY list. Share your progress!

Worked Well	
Try This	
God showed me	

Continue with the program and watch how God continues to show up for you.

Name: **Date:**

Characteristics	
Special Memories	
Thanks	
Area(s) for Prayer	
Scripture Base	

5 2 TY Yay! You decided to continue on. Keep adding to your 52TY list.

Worked Well	
Try This	
God showed me	

Name: **Date:**

Characteristics	
Special Memories	
Thanks	
Area(s) for Prayer	
Scripture Base	

Trust in the Lord to continue on! God's got you. Read Proverbs 3:5-6.

Worked Well	
Try This	
God showed me	

Name: _____ **Date:** _____

Characteristics	
Special Memories	
Thanks	
Area(s) for Prayer	
Scripture Base	

Stand on Philippians 4:6. You can do this!

Worked Well	
Try This	
God showed me	

Name: **Date:**

Characteristics	
Special Memories	
Thanks	
Area(s) for Prayer	
Scripture Base	

Go to week 18 and 35 and write the name of an encouraging song for your future self to meditate on.

Worked Well	
Try This	
God showed me	

Name: **Date:**

Characteristics	
Special Memories	
Thanks	
Area(s) for Prayer	
Scripture Base	

Read John 15:3. Think of some friends to add to your 52TY list.

Worked Well	
Try This	
God showed me	

Name: **Date:**

Characteristics	
Special Memories	
Thanks	
Area(s) for Prayer	
Scripture Base	

Wow! You've reached 10 people already. Can you believe it? Keep up the good work and add 10 more people to your list.

Worked Well	
Try This	
God showed me	

Name: **Date:**

Characteristics	
Special Memories	
Thanks	
Area(s) for Prayer	
Scripture Base	

Be on your guard; stand firm in the faith; be courageous; be strong. 1 Corinthians 16:13 NIV

Worked Well	
Try This	
God showed me	

Name: _____   **Date:** _____

Characteristics	
Special Memories	
Thanks	
Area(s) for Prayer	
Scripture Base	

42 Read Jeremiah 29:11 and meditate on the plans that God has for you regarding 52TY.

Worked Well	
Try This	
God showed me	

Name: **Date:**

Characteristics	
Special Memories	
Thanks	
Area(s) for Prayer	
Scripture Base	

13 ✧ You've reached the ¼ mark and have completed it! Write yourself some encouragement for weeks 23 and 33.

Worked Well	
Try This	
God showed me	

Name: **Date:**

Characteristics	
Special Memories	
Thanks	
Area(s) for Prayer	
Scripture Base	

You are making a difference in the lives of those on your 52TY list.

Worked Well	
Try This	
God showed me	

Name: **Date:**

Characteristics	
Special Memories	
Thanks	
Area(s) for Prayer	
Scripture Base	

15 Read I Peter 2:9.

Worked Well	
Try This	
God showed me	

Name: **Date:**

Characteristics	
Special Memories	
Thanks	
Area(s) for Prayer	
Scripture Base	

Praise God for the victory that is coming with your 52TY journey! Write yourself a note for weeks 36 and 46.

Worked Well	
Try This	
God showed me	

Name: **Date:**

Characteristics	
Special Memories	
Thanks	
Area(s) for Prayer	
Scripture Base	

Therefore, my dear brothers and sisters, stand firm. Let nothing move you. Always give yourselves fully to the work of the Lord, because you know that your labor in the Lord is not in vain. 1 Corinthians 15:58 NIV

Worked Well	
Try This	
God showed me	

Name: **Date:**

Characteristics	
Special Memories	
Thanks	
Area(s) for Prayer	
Scripture Base	

48

Worked Well	
Try This	
God showed me	

Name: **Date:**

Characteristics	
Special Memories	
Thanks	
Area(s) for Prayer	
Scripture Base	

I'm excited about your progress! Write some encouragement for weeks 28 and 37.

Worked Well	
Try This	
God showed me	

Name: **Date:**

Characteristics	
Special Memories	
Thanks	
Area(s) for Prayer	
Scripture Base	

It's always nice to see another balloon. That means that you've completed another 10 people! Yay, YOU!

Worked Well	
Try This	
God showed me	

Name: **Date:**

Characteristics	
Special Memories	
Thanks	
Area(s) for Prayer	
Scripture Base	

I appreciate you moving forward. May God continue to encourage you.

Worked Well	
Try This	
God showed me	

Name: _____   **Date:** _____

Characteristics	
Special Memories	
Thanks	
Area(s) for Prayer	
Scripture Base	

22 Read Lamentations 3:22 – 23.

Worked Well	
Try This	
God showed me	

Name: **Date:**

Characteristics	
Special Memories	
Thanks	
Area(s) for Prayer	
Scripture Base	

23

Worked Well	
Try This	
God showed me	

Name: **Date:**

Characteristics	
Special Memories	
Thanks	
Area(s) for Prayer	
Scripture Base	

24   Shake off any doubts and keep moving forward! Take it one week at a time.

Worked Well	
Try This	
God showed me	

Name: **Date:**

Characteristics	
Special Memories	
Thanks	
Area(s) for Prayer	
Scripture Base	

25 ♪ Your prayers are blessing others. Amen.

Worked Well	
Try This	
God showed me	

Name: _____ **Date:** _____

Characteristics	
Special Memories	
Thanks	
Area(s) for Prayer	
Scripture Base	

26 Halfway through your list of 52 people! Look how far you've come!

Worked Well	
Try This	
God showed me	

Name: **Date:**

Characteristics	
Special Memories	
Thanks	
Area(s) for Prayer	
Scripture Base	

27. Read James 1:2 – 4. Be blessed!

Worked Well	
Try This	
God showed me	

Name: **Date:**

Characteristics	
Special Memories	
Thanks	
Area(s) for Prayer	
Scripture Base	

28

Worked Well	
Try This	
God showed me	

Name: **Date:**

Characteristics	
Special Memories	
Thanks	
Area(s) for Prayer	
Scripture Base	

29 God is giving you strength to continue on. One prayer at a time.

Worked Well	
Try This	
God showed me	

Name: **Date:**

Characteristics	
Special Memories	
Thanks	
Area(s) for Prayer	
Scripture Base	

You've just completed another set of 10 people! Wu-hoo!

Worked Well	
Try This	
God showed me	

Name: **Date:**

Characteristics	
Special Memories	
Thanks	
Area(s) for Prayer	
Scripture Base	

31 Read Romans 8:31 - 39.

Worked Well	
Try This	
God showed me	

Name: **Date:**

Characteristics	
Special Memories	
Thanks	
Area(s) for Prayer	
Scripture Base	

32 God is doing something astonishing with your prayers.

Worked Well	
Try This	
God showed me	

Name: **Date:**

Characteristics	
Special Memories	
Thanks	
Area(s) for Prayer	
Scripture Base	

33

Worked Well	
Try This	
God showed me	

Name: **Date:**

Characteristics	
Special Memories	
Thanks	
Area(s) for Prayer	
Scripture Base	

34 It's incredible to see that you've blessed 34 people already with your gift of intercessory prayer. Keep it going!

Worked Well	
Try This	
God showed me	

Name: **Date:**

Characteristics	
Special Memories	
Thanks	
Area(s) for Prayer	
Scripture Base	

35

Worked Well	
Try This	
God showed me	

Name: **Date:**

Characteristics	
Special Memories	
Thanks	
Area(s) for Prayer	
Scripture Base	

36

Worked Well	
Try This	
God showed me	

Name: **Date:**

Characteristics	
Special Memories	
Thanks	
Area(s) for Prayer	
Scripture Base	

37

Worked Well	
Try This	
God showed me	

Name: **Date:**

Characteristics	
Special Memories	
Thanks	
Area(s) for Prayer	
Scripture Base	

38 Your goal is on the horizon! Every week brings you closer.

Worked Well	
Try This	
God showed me	

Name: **Date:**

Characteristics	
Special Memories	
Thanks	
Area(s) for Prayer	
Scripture Base	

39 You've completed 75% of this journey towards 52 weeks. That's a remarkable accomplishment.

Worked Well	
Try This	
God showed me	

Name: **Date:**

Characteristics	
Special Memories	
Thanks	
Area(s) for Prayer	
Scripture Base	

10-20-30-40 people! You are doing it!

Worked Well	
Try This	
God showed me	

Name: **Date:**

Characteristics	
Special Memories	
Thanks	
Area(s) for Prayer	
Scripture Base	

Devote yourselves to prayer with an alert mind and a thankful heart. Colossians 4:2 NLT

Worked Well	
Try This	
God showed me	

Name: **Date:**

Characteristics	
Special Memories	
Thanks	
Area(s) for Prayer	
Scripture Base	

42 Next week will begin your final 10 people. All I can say is YAAAAAAAAY!

Worked Well	
Try This	
God showed me	

Name: **Date:**

Characteristics	
Special Memories	
Thanks	
Area(s) for Prayer	
Scripture Base	

43 Your words are powerful. Speak life.

Worked Well	
Try This	
God showed me	

Name: **Date:**

Characteristics	
Special Memories	
Thanks	
Area(s) for Prayer	
Scripture Base	

44 God is making a way in someone's life because of your prayers.

Worked Well	
Try This	
God showed me	

Name: **Date:**

Characteristics	
Special Memories	
Thanks	
Area(s) for Prayer	
Scripture Base	

45 Read Psalm 84 focusing on verses 11 and 12. So thankful for God's favor.

Worked Well	
Try This	
God showed me	

Name: **Date:**

Characteristics	
Special Memories	
Thanks	
Area(s) for Prayer	
Scripture Base	

46

Worked Well	
Try This	
God showed me	

Name: **Date:**

Characteristics	
Special Memories	
Thanks	
Area(s) for Prayer	
Scripture Base	

47 The 52TY community is cheering you along as you near your 52!

Worked Well	
Try This	
God showed me	

Name: **Date:**

Characteristics	
Special Memories	
Thanks	
Area(s) for Prayer	
Scripture Base	

48   Alright! You are almost there!

Worked Well	
Try This	
God showed me	

Name: **Date:**

Characteristics	
Special Memories	
Thanks	
Area(s) for Prayer	
Scripture Base	

49 For God is working in you, giving you the desire and the power to do what pleases him. Philippians 2:13 NLT

Worked Well	
Try This	
God showed me	

Name: _____   **Date:** _____

Characteristics	
Special Memories	
Thanks	
Area(s) for Prayer	
Scripture Base	

Always be joyful. Never stop praying. Be thankful in all circumstances, for this is God's will for you who belong to Christ Jesus.
1 Thessalonians 5:16 – 18 NLT

Worked Well	
Try This	
God showed me	

Name: **Date:**

Characteristics	
Special Memories	
Thanks	
Area(s) for Prayer	
Scripture Base	

5:1 ꞋBut grow in the grace and knowledge of our Lord and Savior Jesus Christ. To him be glory both now and forever! Amen. 2 Peter 3:18 NIV

Worked Well	
Try This	
God showed me	

Name: **Date:**

Characteristics	
Special Memories	
Thanks	
Area(s) for Prayer	
Scripture Base	

52   Your persistence, your prayers, and your passion towards being used by God has helped you complete your ENTIRE 52TY list. Congratulations!

Worked Well	
Try This	
God showed me	

praise.

prayer.

thanks!

about

CYNTHIA A. GIPSON LEE

PUTTING DOWN HER PENCIL WITH A TRIUMPHANT THUD, CYNTHIA SAT BACK, PICKED UP HER JUICE BOX, AND ADMIRED THE RECENTLY COMPLETED FLOORPLANS OF HER NEW COMPANY BUILDING.
Being only in elementary school, Cynthia had never heard of a business plan before, but one summer day, with large pieces of construction paper in hand and her imagination towards something other than unicorns and Barbies, she knew that she had a desire to start a fashion design business and began drafting the floorplans. As what seemed to be an activity to pass the long summer days, years later, Cynthia realized this was the start of her entrepreneur's journey.

The passion towards this activity was not around fashion or being a veterinarian, or any of the childhood careers that Cynthia oscillated between but at its root had a heart towards entrepreneurship. Whether it be the pop-up card store that she and her sister started as kids, or making pumpkin bread and gift baskets for her dad's co-workers, or even designing t-shirts for any of the family trips her mom planned, she has always felt a draw towards business.

Cynthia's love of problem solving and logic was a natural pairing for a study in Computer Science, something which both of her parents studied in graduate school. Cynthia received her strong foundation in Computer Science from Morgan State University and later earned her Masters of Science degree from the New Jersey Institute of Technology (NJIT). While at Morgan, she met the love of her life and forever business partner, Chinor Lee. They married and created their FamiLee: Aja, Chinor, and Zacharias.

Cynthia has had a long career in the technology industry as a Software Engineer and has also done work as a corporate trainer, customer service representative, and franchisee (outside the tech field).

Cynthia's second home is her childhood church of First Baptist Church of Lincoln Gardens in Somerset, NJ from where she grew up attending Sunday School and now has been blessed to worship, serve and raise her kids. She has served as part of the Deaconess board, Marriage Ministry, Sunday School, Online Ministry, and wherever needed. She loves family, seeks out fun, and longs to be a blessing and let God use her.

CYNTHIA A. GIPSON LEE IS GOD'S CHILD. UNIQUELY CREATED AND DESIGNED TO BE A BLESSING TO OTHERS; USING WHAT GOD HAS GIFTED HER WITH AND THE EXPERIENCES THAT GOD HAS BROUGHT HER THROUGH.

52 THANK YOUS

In a style similar to that of Paul and his epistles to churches such as Ephesus and Philippi, 52 Thank Yous strives to strengthen relationships through weekly praise, prayer and thanks for those whom God has blessed us with. As a 52er I spend my week praising God for a specific person, praying for them in targeted areas and then sending a note to thank them for blessing me. 52...to live thoughtfully and purposefully every week, every day and every moment. Will you 52?

What an amazing Bible Study Concept! So much to Thank God for and this study helps us to focus on just that! It is a study of intake and a study with action! Thank you Cynthia Gipson Lee.

First Lady Donna Soaries
First Baptist Church of Lincoln Gardens (Somerset, NJ)

Comments from 52TY recipients

BLESSED WEEK 4
Helps me to be focused on recognizing the blessing of others in my life

LOVED WEEK 13
Staying connected on an intimate level with those you love but don't see/interact with on a regular basis

DELIGHTED WEEK 8
A good exercise to reflect on appreciating people that have impacted your life

GRATEFUL WEEK 14
Keeps me from taking what others do for granted

OVERWHELMED WEEK 7
You give out this love and help make someone's day and what you get in return is the satisfaction knowing you took an extra step to be kind, thoughtful, loving

22865258R00076

Made in the USA
Middletown, DE
22 December 2018